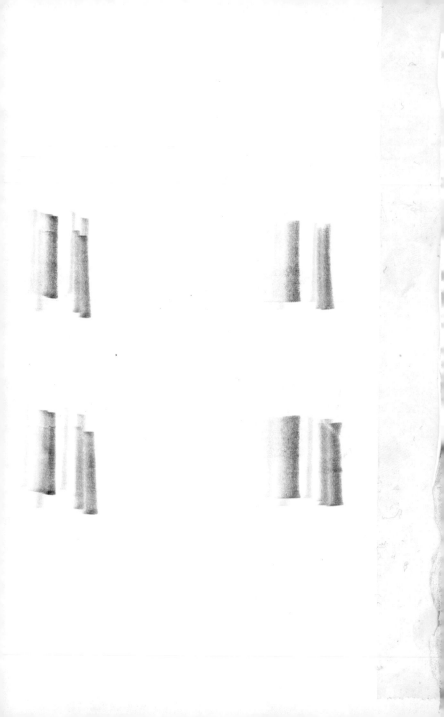

every thought, word, and deed from the perspective of the person I always dreamed I would be.' . . . You inspire!"

"Hearty congratulations on your achievement. You have certainly given me and my life new perspective and focus. Please continue doing what you do best— uplift and inspire to the nth degree!! I thank you for all you have given, all you give today, and all you will continue to give in the future."

"Dear Mike, you are one of the most amazing human beings I've ever come in contact with! I don't know how you do it, but every single e-mail talks to me as if it were written only for me. The messages are exactly what I need to hear all the time. I thank you every day for sharing this gift with me and so many people. I feel truly blessed to have you as a friend, angel, and coach."

"I don't know if I've EVER written a note like this, but I'll wait no longer. To begin the day with a phrase that will be in my heart the entire day, reminding me of who I am and actually knowing that there is a recognition by a fellow traveler of the

# PRAISE FOR MIKE DOOLEY'S NOTES FROM THE UNIVERSE

"For several years I've enjoyed your messages and they never fail to touch my heart. Thanks so much, Mike, for all you do for everyone and yes, especially me. I feel like your messages come to me with heartfelt sincerity . . . and I won't even ask you, 'How DO you do it?' You are obviously well connected."

"Dear Mike, I appreciate your messages. They are like golden nuggets that bless and inspire me. 'Thank you' is an understatement, but I must say it anyway: thank you."

"Mike, you are so awesome! Thanks for sharing your creativity with the world and your humor, and your insights, and your light! You are radiant! I can't tell you how often your 'letters' have put a smile on my face, a bounce in my step, and made me 'reframe beauty of just being on the planet . . . is priceless. The words that are gifted to me and gratefully accepted into my being are the first thing I come to each day. You are a man, you are the 'universe,' you are the proof that a force of good is the only force that is truly effective. Your words, gifted to me each day, affect everything I come into contact with, because I spend the day 're-gifting.'"

"Thank you for the daily words of encouragement. I don't know where you get your material from—I suppose it's from some deeper level of love for humankind. But I really, really, really appreciate them. They are so timely and I look forward each morning to reading them. Your encouragement has helped me to heal in many ways and to take action in my life to achieve the things I want. I am achieving small dreams day by day, and reaching for the bigger ones . . ."

"You do a great job, Mike. You reach a group who are turned off to the word of God, yet thirst for the same understandings. I have to translate often between what you write and what my faith-based Christian church says. It is the identical message, as you probably know. Just different metaphors, different names for the powers within us and around us. If ever there was a time in my life when I needed all the positive input, reinforcement of belief in the goodness of life, and belief that the right thing always happens, it is now. Thanks again for all you do."

"I am so glad to have found you. I am amazed how so very often it seems as though the notes are written JUST FOR ME. You would be surprised how often reading Mike's words brings tears to my eyes because it is SO right on for me and what I am doing at that particular moment. Mike's are the first words I read every morning . . . and reread several times throughout the day. Thank you, Mike, for the work that you do."

"Dear Universe, how can I tell you how much you 'make my day'!!!? I think you are the greatest! Keep up the good work, you have no idea the impact you make on people's lives."

# More Notes from the Universe

## LIFE, DREAMS AND HAPPINESS

### Mike Dooley

**ATRIA** BOOKS
New York London Toronto Sydney

BEYOND WORDS
PUBLISHING

**ATRIA** BOOKS

A Division of Simon & Schuster, Inc.
1230 Avenue of the Americas
New York, NY 10020

BEYOND WORDS

P U B L I S H I N G

20827 N.W. Cornell Road, Suite 500
Hillsboro, Oregon 97124-9808
503-531-8700 / 503-531-8773 fax
www.beyondword.com

First Atria Books/Beyond Words hardcover edition June 2008

**ATRIA** BOOKS and colophon are trademarks of Simon & Schuster, Inc.

Beyond Words Publishing is a division of Simon & Schuster, Inc.

For more information about special discounts for bulk purchases,
please contact Simon & Schuster Special Sales at
1-800-456-6798 or business@simonandschuster.com.

Manufactured in the United States of America

1  3  5  7  9  10  8  6  4  2

Library of Congress Cataloging-in-Publication Data
Dooley, Mike.
More notes from the universe: life, dreams and happiness / Mike Dooley.
       p. cm.
1. Self-help techniques—Miscellanea. 2. Spirituality—Miscellanea.
              3. Occultism—Miscellanea. I. Title.
                  BF1999.D6155    2008
          158—dc22              2007047280

              ISBN-13: 978-1-58270-184-4
              ISBN-10:    1-58270-184-9

The corporate mission of Beyond Words Publishing, Inc.: *Inspire to Integrity*

*For "Bud"*

# INTRODUCTION

Over the past eight years, ever since I began writing the Notes, I've been receiving e-mails and letters of appreciation that have included questions about myself and how I began writing as "The Universe."

Well . . . I'm forty-seven, single, and for the past nineteen years have lived in Orlando, Florida. I haven't always been a writer. Fresh from college, I worked for PricewaterhouseCoopers as a certified public accountant, between their Tampa, Riyadh, and Boston offices. Six years later, I teamed up with my brother (a graphic artist at the time) and my mother (who's always been really cool) to launch a T-shirt line we called TUT, for "Totally Unique T-shirts®." Early on, we discovered our best-selling T-shirt designs were the ones that included our own messages and poems about "life, dreams, and happiness," and after writing a string of "blockbusters," I became our full-time T-shirt writer. Experiencing creativity like this was new to me and thrilling. The idea that something like a poem could be born of thought, to last in time and space longer than myself, was, and still is, intoxicating. My only "complaint" was that I wished I could reach more people with my words than I could by putting them on T-shirts adorned with little fishies and palm trees that were sold primarily to resort markets.

But then came the "train wreck." After ten years of boom time, the trends for TUT began declining so sharply that we ultimately decided to liquidate everything, and get out while the getting was good. Scary, nonetheless.

I was at a loss to explain how I, of all people(!), could have ended up without any career momentum, starting completely over at the age of thirty-nine with absolutely no idea what to do next. Still, I knew I had to move on by defining what I wanted for my life in terms of the "end result" and then physically moving toward it, knocking on every door and turning over every stone. I had no intention of trying to understand the train wreck, because I knew that if I went on some wild-goose chase to find out what was wrong with my life, I would have found plenty!

Alternatively, I had every intention of getting my life going again, as fast as possible.

My end result was to write, speak, and teach about the nature of reality, and be so successful at it that I would live in wealth and abundance, travel the world, and have the most amazing friends to share it all with, though *how* to proceed was daunting. Feeling rather desperate, I simply committed to doing *all* that I could, with what little I had, from where I was, in a never-ending parade of "baby steps," while turning over the "hows" to the Universe. And so began the invisible yet miraculous evolution of serendipities and circumstances that led me to write as "The Universe."

In those first few months of my new adventure, had the idea ever entered my head to simply write as "The Universe," daily, for free, I would have surely rolled over and brushed it off as harebrained. Instead, I worked within my comfort zone and wrote, as myself, "Monday Morning Motivators" (MMMs)—simply, poems taken from one of our T-shirt designs, followed by a few paragraphs of plainspoken but deeply thought-out insight, mailed to those who had signed our guest book in the former retail stores. These were followed later in the week by much briefer "Silver Bullets," little reminders of life's magic, much like today's Notes, sent Tuesday through Friday. The MMMs were popular, but time-consuming to write, and the "Silver Bullets" had to be renamed, or so I was told by my subscribers, since bullets are better known for wreaking havoc than sparking enlightenment.

Happily, as the months rolled by *and I continued writing in spite of these little "speed bumps,"* I became haunted by the idea that I could write more powerfully and from a loftier perspective if I took on the persona of "God," aka "The Universe." And while this, too, seemed foolhardy, it also seemed workable when I realized that I could do it in a playful way. And why not, I thought, for surely the Universe is far more playful than most people give it credit for.

But there was another surprise in store for me as I continued writing, and that was the possibility of injecting humor, which turns out to be *far* easier to achieve when writing as "The Universe" than as plain, old mere-mortal Mike. After all, who cares if some stranger named Mike Dooley says "You rock" or "Cowabunga," but when the words are coming from "The Universe," it's far more likely to catch the reader's eye and bring a smile.

Of course, the Notes are still sent free as e-mails five days a week, fifty-two weeks a year, and never has a single one been repeated, yet eight years ago, when I "knocked on all the doors" and "turned over every stone," insisting only upon my end result and not the "hows," I was also "led" to create audio programs, write books, and give talks around the world. And today, with over 230,000 daily readers who often want to hear more of what I have to share, I'm happy to report that the Universe has indeed taken care of all the "hows," and then some.

Ironically, as I look back over my shoulder to where I was eight years ago, I can't seem to find any remnants of a train wreck. Before the commotion, I wrote about life, dreams, and happiness, yet dreamed of reaching more people. Today, of course, I do both . . . BIG-time. It seems that the train only changed tracks in preparation for the most magical journey of my life so far, yet trying to interpret the commotion from so close, with my physical senses alone, was all but impossible. The scariest thought I have these days is realizing that if I had spent that time eight years ago trying to figure out what was wrong with my life, you and I never would have met.

To the life of *your* dreams,

# HOW YOU MIGHT
# USE THIS BOOK

---

When these Notes were first sent out by e-mail to subscribers, the most common reply I received (and still receive, endlessly) was that more often than not, day after day, readers were amazed by the uncanny timing of each Note as it related to exactly where they were in their respective lives. "How could you know? Even my closest friends don't have a clue!" Or "I was eating French toast at 4 a.m. when today's Note arrived . . . and I *had* to call and wake my mother to share that the PS asked, 'More syrup?' just as I was reaching for it!" Or "As I was worrying about the sad ending of my marriage and its potential effect on my children, tears and tissues everywhere, today's Note arrived telling me, 'If you only knew just how incredibly well everything is going to turn out for you and those close to you, right now you'd likely feel light as a feather, free as the wind, happy, confident, giddy . . .'"

How, indeed? The obvious answer is that while

230,000 people receive the exact same Note, none of them interprets it the same way; each reader filters it through his or her own thoughts and circumstances. The not-so-obvious answer is that in the jungles of time and space, things are *not* as they appear. We've been told since our lives began that we are but mere bystanders to the glory of life and that everything happens along a rigid, linear time line. The truth, however, is that we're each the co-creator of all that we share, and our experiences spring from an eternal now. It's only our exclusive reliance upon our physical senses to interpret life that makes this so challenging to grasp. And so, just as those who witness a beautiful sunrise actually *participate* in its creation, so, too, in some mystical, magical way are the readers of these words and the daily Notes their co-creators—whether they were received as an e-mail in the "past" or randomly chosen from the pages now before you.

Go on, give it a try. Just open this book to any "random" page and see what you get. You're really quite the writer, you know.

# So-o-o-o-o-o-o . . .

*How's it going down on earth?*
*You know—in time and space, where thoughts become*
*things, all things are possible, and dreams come true?!*
*Are you totally kicking butt?*

*Oh, I see . . .*

*Yikes . . .*

*Uh-huh . . .*

*Oh dear . . .*

*You don't say . . .*

*Psssst . . . I want to let you in on a little secret:*

*Everyone has issues.*

*Everyone. Even those who don't appear to. Because*
*without issues, nothing would be worthwhile.*

*Think about that.*

*So glad we have these little talks . . .*

*The Universe*

# Notes

from the

# Universe

# Of course you sometimes feel

alone, confused, and frightened! You come from an ancient spiritual family of the finest imaginable lineage, loved and respected by all. They threw the happiest parties, knew the happiest souls, and lived in mansions of solid gold. They were so adored and respected throughout the cosmos that whatever they wanted, they received twelve times over.

You, however . . . Wellll, it's like when it came time for your education and the furthering of your divine awareness, you just had to go far, far away. To the most remote little school ever heard of, deep within the jungles of time and space, called *Earth*.

Created quite the stir, you did. Until, of course, you began sending home postcards from the sleep state. Now, as you might have guessed, they toast your name every single night in total awe of your courage.

Me, too.

*You hooligan.*

I have to tell you
that one of the greatest things about being
the Universe is knowing absolutely everything.
Well, that, and making dreams come true. I also
love being eternal. And having no limits. Creating
worlds simply with thought. Knowing that reality
is unfolding just exactly as it should. Having it
all, being it all, doing it all. And I like being
perpetually in love, and loved.

How 'bout you? What's your favorite thing about
being the Universe?

xxxxxxxxxxxxxxxxx ooooooooooooooooo!

There's no predicament
that can't be turned into an advantage.
No foe who can't become a friend.
And no burden that cannot give you wings.

*How fair is that?*

# Now, as the Universe

I don't like telling anyone what they should or shouldn't do. But when the urge arises, I proceed in the most delicate, gentle, and loving way possible:

You look radiant this morning! Did you enjoy our dreams last night concerning the changes and manifestations you want? Have you had a chance to paint a lovely picture in your mind of the "end result"? Are you moving toward what you want, however you can, whenever you can? Are faith and expectation part of your daily constitution? These things are really quite important, you know. Actually, to effect any kind of change at all, honey . . . don't even think there might be another way!

xxoo,

The Universe

*There are some things, dearest, only you can do.*

# You do know what
they're going to do, don't you?

And you do know what they're going to say?

Yeah, once you consistently spend some time visualizing every day, doing the "all you can with what you've got" dance, and pushing yourself to live the life of your dreams to any degree that you now can, so that the floodgates fly open and you have your dream home, your dream work, and your dream friends.

They're gonna give you that long, cold glance out of the corner of their eyes and say in a low, drawn-out voice, just loud enough for you to hear,

"Must . . . be . . . nice . . ."

Just warning you,

The Universe

*And you'll pause, look at them sympathetically, and say, "Oh, actually you get used to it."*

Nothing you will ever do,
be, or have, no matter how stunning and
spectacular, will ever compare to your achievement
of being here at all.

Yes, *your* achievement.

*Amazing, though, how people will put off celebrating
the big stuff for the little stuff.*

*Don't wait.*

Ever wonder why you
sometimes feel like you're on top of your game?
Ever wonder why you sometimes feel so safe, secure,
and deeply loved? Ever wonder why there are days
when you feel invincible, unstoppable, and . . .
well, like

"King of the World"?

Actually, Your Highness, I often wonder why you
don't always have those feelings.

Impressed beyond belief,

The Universe

*I loved that part in* Titanic.

Believe it or not,
if it weren't for your so-called issues, problems,
and challenges, there'd be no other way you could
become even happier, cooler, and more enlightened
than you have ever been before.

*Granted, you being even cooler boggles the mind.*

It's as if you're pounding
on the massive doors of the Kingdom of your
Wildest Dreams. At first lightly, even respectfully.
Then, losing patience, louder and louder.
You pray, you plead, you beg, you ask, you cry,
you wail. And just on the other side of the door,
your faithful, adoring subjects silently writhe,
some quietly crying, all intensely feeling your
frustration and loneliness. Yet they remember
all too well how on the day you left, you made
them swear to not ever open the door so that
you might discover, yourself . . .
that it was left unlocked.

# The perfection

of your every "issue" is beyond your comprehension. Don't be fooled. You've made no mistakes. The territory behind you and the challenges at hand were precisely crafted to deliver the wisdom and insights that will make possible the life of your dreams.

Get through what you must get through today, understand what troubles you, do what you can, and all the rest will be made easy.

You didn't come here to face hurdle after hurdle after hurdle. It doesn't work like that. It's not as if by mastering your issues today, more will be added tomorrow. (That only happens when you deny them today.) Master your issues today, and be free.

*So little can yield so much. A new perspective, an admission, a surrender to truth—however painful— changes everything.*

One hundred years from now,
it will not matter what your bank account was,
what kind of car you drove, or what style of home
you lived in.

On the other hand, since one of the reasons you're
in time and space is to understand that you do,
indeed, have dominion over all things—nailing these
early on would be way cool.

*And what better way to be important in the eyes of
children than to live your power so that they might
observe and learn to live theirs?*

You want what you want
because you know it's possible. If it wasn't,
you wouldn't. This is powerful. Embrace it.
For whatever else you believe or don't believe,
this belief alone can take you the distance.

Please, want what you want.

*Dreams don't come that can't be won.*

So I was talking with this tree
a while back. "Universe . . ." it said to me.

"Yeah?"

"When I come back, I don't want to be just wood."

"Well," I thought aloud, "what's wrong
with being wood?"

"It's hard," the tree said, without cracking a smile.
"When I come back, I want to be soft and furry so
that I'll be loved by children."

And I thought . . . and thought . . . and
thought . . . and finally asked, "Why not be tall and
strong, just as you are, and loved by children?"

And the children came to play.

*Do you really think you have to change
to have what you want?*

The thing about pessimism . . .
about fearful thoughts . . . about limiting
beliefs . . . is that they really, really work.

Boo,

The Universe

*Now, that's about as scary as things get
in time and space!*

# Sometimes life
is like reading a book.

Days, weeks, even years just repeat
themselves . . . until you turn the page.

*Letting go isn't giving up.*
*It's understanding that the best is yet to come.*

# Remember that day

not so long ago, just before you took your
first big gulp of air?

Sure, you remember . . . You were just a wispy
thought and you vowed with clenched teeth and
tight fists (figuratively), "This time I won't forget!
This time I'll remember! This time, no matter how
easy or difficult life gets, I'll refuse to look to the
world around me for meaning, direction, or to
invoke change, knowing instead that the world
around me only mirrors all that moves within my
heart and soul. This time, for meaning, direction, or
to invoke change, I'll go within. All things are
possible. Hip-hop, Scooby-Doo!"

Kind of odd, but you said it.

Oh, yes you did, who else talks like that?

I do not.

*Kind of makes you wonder what happened last time,
doesn't it?*

# It hasn't always been this easy
being the Universe. Before you came along,
I was a lot less.

Before you came along, there was no one who ever thought like you now think. No one who ever felt what you now feel. And perhaps what I treasure most, no one who's ever possesed your priceless view of reality as you now perceive it. And all of these things who have been added unto me.

Thank you, you've done enough. You are enough.

I am so pleased, you have no idea.

With love and adoration,

The Universe

*Of course, my job would be easier still if you could see what I see—in you. This week, let's look together.*

# Happiness isn't a crop

that you harvest when your dreams come true.
It's more like the fertilizer that makes them
come true, faster.

Go ahead, want it all.
Just learn to be happy before it arrives,
or you may not notice when it does.

*Hurry! It won't be long!*

## Perception Management
### for Very Advanced Souls

The next time someone upsets you, think,
"Thanks for pointing out that I've begun depending
on you. Time I lose the expectations."

And the next time someone doesn't take
your view into account, think, "That's okay,
I was once like that."

And if someone steals from you, think, "It was
nothing, my supply is the Universe."

Or lies to you, think, "I'm sorry you feel that need."

Violates you, "All for my growth and glory."

Is rude to you, "Cheer up, dear soul, it'll be okay."

Judges you . . . "Thanks for sharing your truth."

Drives by you like a "bat out of hell" . . .
"Be careful, my friend. I love you."

And the next time someone greets you with a smile,
smile back, like you're sharing a secret.

*Oh, sure, there are other ways to deal with
each scenario. And Very Advanced Souls know
that they're all okay.*

As surely as the snow falls,
the winds rage, and the rivers run, so are you,
minute by minute, day by day, inevitably drawn
to all your heart desires.

*Sure beats thinking that you're just getting older.*

# Yes! Yes! Yes!

Oh-h-h-h-h, y-e-s-s-s-s-s-s!

No. No. No. Not what you're thinking!

(But glad you're coming out of your shell.)

Just answering every single one of the requests I receive. And the "Ohhhhhh, yesssssss!" was for the chap who didn't ask, but who gave thanks in advance.

This may be hard to believe, but I never say no.

Whatever you want,

The Universe

PS—The "No. No. No." doesn't count.

*Do you have any idea how many times a day I say, "Yes!" when the request is clear? Actually, there isn't a number big enough to give you the slightest idea.*

The novice learns to be honest
with others, in terms of who, what,
when, and where.

The advanced soul learns to be honest with self, and
discovers "perspective" rules, yet changes swiftly.

The Master, however, studies honesty in terms
of motivation, where heretofore the lies have
really piled up!

So . . . what do you really, really, really want,
and why?

*Being a Master can be a bear, huh?*

# What a day!

I feel so great, so magnanimous, so everywhere!
Tell you what, today . . . dreams are on me.
Today everyone's dreams will come true!

Can I do that? Gimme a break.

I do it every single day, for everyone, everywhere,
no matter what. Always, second to second, month
to month, year to year, I give you what you think
about, what you most expect, what you believe in
and move toward.

What else are Universes for?

*And soon we shall see, literally,
the thoughts you choose today.*

# You're thanking me?!

No. Sorry. I'm afraid you were misinformed.

You see, it's me who thanks you, every moment of every day, for all that you are.

You have no idea.

*Thank you, thank you, thank you.*

Those feelings you most want
aren't going to come from somewhere new,
someone special, or something wonderful.

Doesn't work like that.

They're going to come from within,
where they now wait for permission to be released—
often in terms of somewhere new, someone special,
or something wonderful.

Chic-a-boom,

The Universe

*Whatever you hope to feel in the future,
you can decide to feel right now.*

Do you think gravity
has to work twice as hard to hold an elephant
to the ground as it does an acorn?

*Ha.*

So please understand, it's the same with
the princple of "thoughts become things."
The size of your dreams has nothing to do with
the likelihood of them coming to pass,
nothing.

Think BIG.

# Now! Go! Stake your claim!

Hold out your hands. Move, get ready, give thanks.
Imagine, and let go. Act, and have faith. Persist.
Do what you can, when you can, all you can.
Because never again, not in a million years, not over
ten thousand lifetimes, will you ever again be as
close as you are today.

Ungawwa,

The Universe

From an endless sea
of wistful souls who've waited out eternity, it's now
your turn, in time and space. And there are simply
no words that can express just how uniquely special
this privilege is.

*Nor how fleeting.*

Waiting for your life to take off?

That could be the problem.

Today there are "likelihoods,"
no concretes, no absolutes, nothing predestined
or set in stone, just "likelihoods." And the ones
that will come to pass *will all pivot* on you
and your thoughts.

You're *that* powerful.

Ever stop to realize
that it's impossible to feel true unconditional
love for any single person, until you can feel it for
every single person?

After all, what differentiates them,
except conditions?

Of course, it doesn't hurt to try.

*Yes, even the clods.*

You wanna know what the single toughest thing about figuring out time and space is? About finally making progress by leaps and bounds with the life of your dreams? The one thing that would heal every broken heart and vanquish every emotional pain? That would clear the way for infinite abundance, perfect health, and unlimited happiness?

Not relying on appearances.

Now, you wanna know the easiest and simplest way to lick 'em?

Stop relying on appearances.

Just stop it.

*You can.*

It's easy.

*Really* easy.

All of it.

It's all *really* easy.

It's a matter of switching gears,
never looking back, and being the person today
that you've always dreamed you'd be.

Entertain every thought, say every word, and make
every decision from their point of view. Walk the
way they would walk, dress the way they would
dress, and spend your free time the way they would
spend theirs. Choose the friends they would choose,
eat the meals they would eat, and love and
appreciate yourself the way they would.

These steps must come in order for there to be
change. There's no other option, no other way.

But . . . since that person is who you really are,
that makes this assignment downright effortless.

Just stop being who you aren't.

Love,

The Universe

Just wanted to let you know
that everyone here is rooting for you.

## Yikes! I'm freakin'!

The holidays aren't far off and I have no idea
what to get for eight billion people this year!

Do you have any idea how difficult it is shopping for
folks who already have dominion over all things?

*There's nothing I can give them
that they can't give themselves.*

# What if today
you could wipe the slate clean, start over,
and write your own ticket?

No. Wait. Let's change that. What if every day
you could wipe the slate clean, start over,
and write your own ticket?

How many days would have to go by before
you discovered that your "slate" and your "ticket"
have nothing to do with each other? That your past
need not live in your future?

*Your absolute freedom and total power lie
in the present moment.*

# S-h-h-h-h-h-h!

Don't say a word and off with the lights!

Now is as good a time as any to watch *It's a Wonderful Life*. No, no, not the one with Jimmy Stewart! The other one! You know . . . starring you. It's the best. A total-underdog, goose-bump, come-from-behind kind of adventure. And what an "ending"!

Whooo-hoooo!

I especially love the part where you, in spite of all evidence to the contrary, finally declare "enough is enough" (actually, far more colorful language is used because we don't have a rating system here) and you begin visualizing, putting up dream photos on the computer, refrigerator, and mirrors, and start performing simple acts of faith, as if your dreams had already come true, every single bloomin' day.

The transformation that follows really pushes the envelope on believability. Except, of course, it's a true story!

It's also a great psych-up "watch" for new souls. You know, before their first big plunge.

Definitely two thumbs-up.

Shhhh . . . The best part is just now starting. You're about to do all that you can do, with what you've got, from where you are, and then turn it over to . . . the Universe! (My second-favorite character.)

You have nothing to fear,
not even fear itself. Because in the final analysis,
you will find your way, you will be delivered,
and your every cup will overflow forever more.

This is set in stone.

*Man . . . Fear, fear, fear! People sure love to scare
others by telling them not to fear fear.*

*Ha!*

# I'm soooooo excited!

Everything's just about ready. I've arranged for all the right players to appear at all the right times. Big shots, little shots, and some absolute angels. (You aren't even going to believe who you'll soon be schmoozing with. Or where!) I've lined up the necessary phone calls, e-mails, and chance encounters so that you'll be disposed to waves of loving, inspired thoughts precisely when most needed. I've calculated—literally to the billionth degree—the pivotal coincidences, happy accidents, and clutch plays that will blast you to heights previously unimagined. Even took care of "happily-ever-after."

*So . . . how are things coming on your end?*

# And the day will come

when you will ask, "Whatever have I done to be so deserving of the friends, laughter, and abundance that now surround me?"

And, of course, I will answer, "You rose to the challenge of seeing yourself as divine and worthy, even while the rest of the world, at first, saw you as neither. And you prevailed."

Well done, maestro. Well done, indeed.

The Universe

How quickly would you like
to be surrounded by wealth and abundance?
Have even more friends and enjoy more laughter?
How fast would you like to grow a thriving business,
or have your own fabulous house on the water?

If you answered "pronto," "ASAP," or "Duh" to any
or all of these questions, could it be that you've
momentarily forgotten that the absolute fastest way
to manifest change is to claim that you already have
it? To withdraw your attention from the yearning?
To think, speak, and act "as if"?

*I didn't think so.*

The very same magic,
the very same, that you used to get your first job,
to find a best friend, and to heal what hurt, that
even now finishes your sentences, beats your heart,
and inspires your dreams, is the exact same "grade"
of stuff that can make what you most want today
come to pass.

Point being: You've already engaged it.
You've already commanded it. You've already
done the bloody impossible!

So what's the big deal about doing it again?

*Oh, go on . . .*

You might not readily believe
this, it might even spook you a bit, but there
are those (actually, far more than you could ever
guess) who chose this very lifetime, in large part,
knowing you'd be there.

*Now, that's what we call a reputation.*

Those folks who find success,
and then tell the world it was due to their hard
work, really make my job challenging. They almost
never work harder than others. They don't even
work smarter than others. They simply engaged
the magic by thinking, speaking, and acting in line
with what they wanted.

But oh, no, they have to go out and tell
impressionable minds that it was their hard
work. And when those minds "buy it" the bar
is raised for them.

*Do yourself a favor, engage the magic.*

To touch someone
with kindness is to change someone forever.

Heavy, huh? That's nothing.

Because for everyone you touch, you also reach
everyone they will ever know. And everyone they
will ever know. And everyone they will ever know.
And so, for the rest of all time, your kindness
will be felt, in waves that will spread,
long after you move on.

*Muchas gracias,*

The Universe

*Don't ask what happens on a "bad" day.*

Everyone's kind
to people they like.

Big whoop-dee-do!

"Roger!" You have been heard.

And at this very moment, every single atom in the cosmos is being reprogrammed, every single angel is being summoned, and big wheels are a-turning.

We just hope you weren't kidding.

*You're always heard. Every single thought.*

# Okay, let's try this . . .

Ever stop and realize that if there was no such thing as time and space, your thoughts would instantaneously manifest before you?

Thought so. Very good. You understand that in such a reality, there'd be no lag or delay as I jockeyed the players, events, and circumstances of your life into place.

Now, in such a reality, it would also be pretty easy to see that there'd be no outside, non-you factors, influencing, guiding, or directing the manifestations that occurred in your experience. Right? You'd simply choose your thoughts, and presto!

All right, then, if you suddenly added the parameters of time and space to this reality, can you still see that there needn't be any outside, non-you factors, influencing, guiding, or directing the manifestations that occur all around you? That if there were, you wouldn't have dominion over all things? Can you see, that under no circumstances would anything, ever, be predestined or "meant to be"? Not relationships, not jobs, not nothin'?

Further, can you see that any such hypothetical predetermined destinies would severely limit your ability to create your own reality, stifle your creativity, and make "null and void" the inviolate, universal principle of "thoughts becoming things"?

Excellent! Because that brings us to today and the morals behind this lesson:

1. Absolutely anything can happen in time and space, if you dream it up first.

2. Positively nothing will happen in time and space, if you don't.

3. Lags and delays should never be cause to assume something isn't meant to be. They're just the cloaks and curtains I must work behind.

*And, dearest, if you could see what I now see moving behind your curtain, you'd never, ever, settle for less than exactly what you most want.*

To clear up a little something:
When it comes to your every cup overflowing . . .

Yes, I thought you'd remember
that one.

Well, we neglected to add it's a self-service "bar."

*But isn't that better than having to ask,*
*wait, and hope?*

# How ever do you do it?

You know, talk, and make such sense? Walk, and not fall down? Ask, and then know the answer? Aim, and then deliver? Show up on time? Always get by? Make just enough?

How on earth?!

You don't know how, do you?

You haven't got a clue.

And that's exactly how you do it.

You leave the details, the "hows," to Me—as you simply focus upon and move toward the end result. Expectant, even.

*Dreams come true the same way.*

# Would you believe

that there are some people who actually think they can change their life through "pretending it better"?

Yep! And we call them Masters.

In awe of you,

The Universe

*Sure beats pretending nothing is happening. Ha!*

When it comes to others,
rather than wishing they were somehow different,
it's better to give thanks that they are exactly as they
are, because truly, if they weren't, they wouldn't
even be in your life right now.

Always take the high road.

And I'll see you there.

### Friends and partners
to celebrate life with, abundance to enhance
any adventure, and mountains to perch atop all
arrive when you dwell upon the celebration, the
adventure, and the view. Not names, lotteries,
or the path you think wisest.

This is so important—
because I want you to have them all.

*Yes, you can have whatever you want, anything.
Just please don't confuse what you want with how
you're going to get it.*

How'd you like a little peek
into the future? Oh, I really shouldn't, but,
well, you so rock, I figure this indulgence,
just once, will be all right.

You're sitting around a warm and cozy fireplace
surrounded by friends and boisterous laughter.
Early-morning snow gently falling across the
countryside is visible from the enormous,
ceiling-high windows beside you. Everyone is
sipping hot chocolate and reminiscing about the
fabulous circumstances that have brought you
together, brimming with excitement for times
ahead. And then you chime in, "If only I'd seen it,
I would never have been so hard on myself.

If only I'd had just the slightest inkling that the challenges, lacks, and issues I faced back then were of my own exacting design, and that they'd soon make possible the whirlwind of events that so swiftly followed, I'd have been . . . well, as proud of myself back then as I am now."

And then your friends all start clapping.

Not a word to anyone.

*You're also wearing the most outrageous sparkly tights I've ever seen. But then, you always could wear anything.*

"Reality" is not
that you are weak, and dream of becoming strong.
Poor, and dream of becoming rich. Alone, and
dream of having friends. But that you're already
strong, rich, and among friends. Yet, at times,
dream that you're not.

# No matter what your faith is,

or is not. No matter where in the world you are. I want you to know, I'll be with you. Behind the eyes of every child, and in the melody of every song, I'll be the glimmer in the ice crystals, the rays in the sun, and the stars at night.

And with each smile you see, every hug you receive, and every laugh you hear, I'll be there reaching out through another, with blessings and tidings to last you the year, because I love you. Because I've always loved you. And because I always will. And because this has been true, and will be true, every day of your life.

Blessings to you, to your family, and to every single wonderful, radiant Being in your shimmering, enlightened sphere.

*Remember this, and be sure to look for me—*
*all year long.*

# There comes a time

in the evolution of every spiritual being,
along that sometimes dark road that leads to
enlightenment, when their inner yearnings,
struggles, and frustrations bring them to a truth
that could not otherwise have been achieved.
And so, dearly beloved, I come this sacred day
with such a truth, though it may temporarily hurt
eyes that have been shut too long. Reaching this
milestone was inevitable, for the light that will
dawn hereafter is not only what you have
summoned, but what all now seek. And with
your blessing and recognition, it will bathe those
who follow in your footsteps and the burden
they bear shall be lessened.

A more perfect child of the Universe has never
existed. Until now, only a celebration cloaked in
myth and mystery could hint at your sublime
heritage and divine destiny. You are life's prayer of

becoming, and its answer. The first light at the dawn of eternity, drawn from the ether, so that the Universe might know its depths, discover its heights, and frolic in endless seas of blessed emotion.

A pioneer into illusion, an adventurer into the unknown, and a lifter of veils. Courageous, heroic, and exalted by countless souls in the unseen.

To give beyond reason. To care beyond hope. To love without limit. To reach, stretch, and dream in spite of fear. These are the hallmarks of divinity— traits of the immortal—your badges of honor, and your ticket home.

This is the time of year we celebrate who you are.

The Universe

*Hmmmm . . . Think I should switch to decaf?*

Contrary to popular thinking,
being worthy isn't something you earn, it's
something you recognize.

And once you do, you won't be able to think,
speak, or behave in any other way than as if what
you most wanted, was meant to be.

And so it shall be, because truly there's no one
worthier than you.

Thinking big but acting small,
is the same as thinking small.

Shiver me timbers.

*Reading this and nodding in wholehearted agreement,
but not doing a little acting "as if your dreams have
come true" in the days that follow, is the same as not
reading this.*

## Let's just say

you're driving down the road listening to some hip-hop, happy kind of music. Then, after a while, you decide you want to hear something else, maybe some classic rock. Would you just hope that the hip-hop station starts playing rock? Would you visualize it, and say, "YES! I believe in the magic! I know that thoughts become things! I can 'see' the Boss now, I can 'hear' the E Street Band. Thank you, Universe, in advance, thank you, thank you, thank you. I am so grateful!"?

Or after thinking about what you wanted, would you change the station?

Good. Just checking.

Rock on,

The Universe

# When life hurts.

When it baffles and confuses. When it doesn't
quite seem to work. These are just signs from Me,
as if I were tapping on your shoulder or whispering
in your ear, trying to point out that something
important, something really, really important,
is being misunderstood.

Actually, while it's fun
to think about how fantastically different life
will be once your ship comes in, the truth is,
the only thing that will really change, is you.

*Hey, why wait?*

# I don't quite know

if it's the way your mind works, or your emotional sensitivity. I don't know if it's the way you laugh, or the way you cry. Could be your tenacity and courage. Or maybe it's your wit and spontaneity. Truth is there's never been anyone like you, so it's hard to tell. But whatever it is, to me, from here, right now, you sure improve the view.

You are soooo beautiful.

Gratefully,

The Universe

# I'm everywhere . . .

Between the bombs, beside each soldier, and in the racing hearts of every combatant, I now reside joyfully radiant. Knowing that an unfolding war, like all catastrophes, will ultimately serve to awaken your spirit, draw you together, and inspire an everlasting compassion as you begin to finally realize that the glint in your enemy's eye . . . was only a tear.

You know how sometimes
when you visualize, you end up daydreaming, too?

Or when you finally remember to perform
an act of faith, it feels kind of hokey?

Or sometimes you catch yourself worrying,
or thinking too much about the past,
or wondering whether or not you have
invisible limiting beliefs holding you back?

Well, that's exactly what all Illuminates go
through (especially the good-looking ones).
But they arrive in spite of it, and so will you.

Worry not; just keep chugging.

Hugs,

The Universe

No, not as in *gulp, gulp,* as in *choo, choo.*

All right, you know how in golf,
when you play with a friend and they hit
the ball really, really close to the cup, only a
stroke away from sinking it, you say, "Great shot,
that's a 'gimme'!" (Meaning you're not going to
make them putt the next one, because they'd
probably make it, so you just give it to them?)
Just say, "Yes."

Right!

Well, about your dreams . . . The good news
is that they're so close to manifesting that in
golf they'd be "gimmes"!

*Right again! This ain't golf . . .
and it's your turn.*

There are lots of people
out there whose lives would be made "richer,"
if only they'd "let you in."

*And perhaps, vice versa?*

The thing to remember,
to always remember, is that what you do,
or don't do, today, is what matters most.

In fact, nothing else does.

# If it weren't for your challenges,
how would you ever know that there are
things you still misunderstand?

You wouldn't.

Bless them. Embrace them. Give thanks.

*Oh, sure. I could just tell you.*
*Ha, ha, ha, ha, ha, ha, ha,*
*haaa . . . Ehee . . . OOHHAAHAAA . . .*
*HE-HE-HE-HE-HE! WHO-HA!*
*That was a good one!*

# Okay, you're sitting

in a little room, staring out the only window
you've ever known, at a world that's so incredibly
beautiful you can hardly believe your good fortune.
Every night you draw the blinds to sleep and every
sunrise you rush to the window to gaze some more.
Your life is idyllic.

Now, let's just say, one day while gazing out
the window at the wondrous, lush, enchanting
paradise you've come to love, something incredible
happens. Bulldozers appear, workers descend,
and construction begins on a huge, gigantic
chicken statue that destroys your view.

Assuming you've never had a fondness for
chicken statues, what would you do next?

A. Learn to love the chicken statue,
since it is "of God," too?

B. Live off the memory of what used to be?

C. Call a lawyer and begin litigation?

D. Pick up your chair and move to another little
room with a totally different view, in your
incredible, magical mansion?

No. Just one answer, please.

You're beautiful enough.

You're special enough.

You're sexy, playful, and fun enough.

You've worked enough.

You've cried enough.

You've been grateful, generous, and kind enough.

Okay, then? So what are you waiting for?

Give it to yourself!

Your faithful scorekeeper,

The Universe

*You see, I'm not the one who needs convincing.
Nor am I the one who's holding it back.*

# Ahha! Found you, didn't I?

Dreaming you're human again.
Can't blame you. What a blast! You really know
how to craft an adventure! I bet they'll even
name a few bridges, or towns, or ponies after
you in a couple hundred years!

Well, sorry to interrupt. As you were. Stay in touch,
and be careful not to let all those adventures go to
your head. Remember, nine out of ten angels
temporarily lose themselves "dreaming human,"
because they begin taking everything so dang
seriously.

*Hey, you're good-looking this time!*

# Met up with the dearest

little angel over the weekend, but she was so, so sad.

She asked, in the sweetest of angel voices, how there could be so much love in the world, yet so few feel it. How there could be so much beauty, yet hardly anyone sees it. And how there could be so many miracles, yet most go unrecognized.

Poor thing.

So I reminded her of something far more important. I reminded her that whether or not one knows of the love, one is still bathed in it. Whether or not one sees the beauty, one still adds to it. And whether or not one recognizes the miracles, one still performs them, every single day.

Then, we both just beamed.

*And whether or not these things are now known, they will be, by all.*

# If you want it, I got it.

I got it! So why look elsewhere? To others?
To the things of time and space? Aren't we one?

Yes. Do your earthly things. Do all of them.
Move with your dreams. Not because of what you
may or may not achieve, but because you love life . . .
Because you'll thereby exponentially increase the
opportunities I have to share what's ours and
because . . . you can.

*After all, you are why "I got it."*

It doesn't matter what "they" do.

Your net worth, net health, and net happiness all hinge exclusively upon your net thoughts, net words, and net deeds. Though little can rob you as quickly as thinking that it matters what "they" do.

*You've got the power.*

# Consider, if you will,
## an enlightened soul.

Does Kwai Chang Caine of *Kung Fu*
come to mind? Certainly a likable chap,
meditating and all that.

Now picture this: a being so alive that his
vibrations heighten all of his senses. His energy
effortlessly summoning circumstances, gathering
friends, and blasting limits. Falling so in love
with the adventure of life that, like a child on a
playground, he can't help but stretch, reach, and
rediscover all of his capabilities. Wanting to be
involved in every "game." Yearning to spring
from bed each morning to greet the day. Dipping
his toes in every pool, stream, and ocean, simply
because he can. Understanding the power of

thought, and then sailing out into the world to avail himself of its magic. Knocking on every door and turning over every stone to facilitate the swift manifestation of his dreams.

Sure, you can do less and have more once you're enlightened. But when you realize that the world spins in your very hand, that your thoughts become the things and events of your life, and that there's truly nothing you can't do, be, or have, who would want to do less?

Have at it, Grasshopper,

The Universe

*I know! How about a new TV series to improve enlightenment's image:* Gods Gone Wild?

# Argggg!

Oh, hi, doing a little accounting here.
Universe stuff, you know. Kind of like your tax
time. Sheeeezz . . . All these debits and credits!
Hard to make heads or tails of 'em. I've got a little
quota system here for doling out wealth, abundance,
friends, love, laughter . . . you name it. Says here
you signed up for "it all," but I've hardly
given you your share.

Hmmm . . . Tell me . . . Are you coming to me
for these things? Leveraging the Universe and
engaging the magic? Or are you trying to muster
them up on your own . . . ?

Perhaps the most exciting
realization in the world is finally understanding that
living the life of your dreams is entirely up to you.

It's also about the scariest.

*Until you realize that "you" includes "Me."*

# I have a confession to make.

You know those folks in your life who you
kind of wish weren't in your life?

Well . . . they're plants.

No, not the green, leafy kind. You know, stooges.
Like "plants" in an audience. People placed
there as if to test you.

I know, I know, I shouldn't have, but . . .
that's how much I love you.

The test is to not let them bug you. Can you do
that? If you can, I'll either normalize them or pull
'em out like weeds, as you prefer. Otherwise they
stay put, or worse, start multiplying like spring rye
watered with Miracle-Gro.

Of course, I wouldn't have planted them in the first
place if you hadn't insisted. And the test analogy?
That was just an analogy.

*If you tell them I said the weed thing, the deal's off.*

Getting what you think about,
being loved and adored, and having the
whole world spin in the palm of your hand
aren't things you learn, earn, or force.

Breathing is enough.

*Because you already do, you already are,
and it already does.*

# You're simply the best.

You blow my mind. We're all in total awe.
How you hold together under pressure. How you
face up to your challenges. And your rebound ability
totally rocks. You're driven, persistent, and strong.
Playful, silly, fun. Compassionate, sympathetic,
understanding. You're just plain unstoppable.
And you always have time for others.
What a package. Soooo . . .

How 'bout cutting yourself some slack
every now and then?

# What a cool party, huh?!

Ever see so many happy, smiling faces dancing
around like they don't have a care in the world?
The food's from New Orleans. The chef from Paris.
And the dancers are Bohemians! And how about all
those helicopters and yachts bringing everyone to
the island? What a trip! Hey, it's kind of loud here,
let's go down to the pool . . . No, the other pool,
by the tiki torches and palm trees so we don't
have to compete with the bongo drums.

That's better. Now that I have your attention, and
before we get swept away in the next conga line, I
want to thank you. Thank you for being such an
incredible example, and of course, thank you for
inviting me to your party! You've really outdone
yourself, again. Your home here is spectacular, your
friends are a blast, and . . . Oh my "God"! Isn't that
Mick Jagger singing?! *You* know Mick Jagger?!

By the way, what are we celebrating this time?

*Get used to it.*

Fear just means
you've forgotten how deeply you're loved,
how safe you are, and that happiness will return,
like you've never known it before.

It doesn't change these things.

# Nothing is ever lost

in this adventure of all adventures. The lessons and discoveries of every single life, no matter how large or small, difficult or easy, are added to the whole. Like stones in the base of a pyramid, they permanently raise, and forever support every manner of adventure that follows. And so it is that the hearts of those who came first continue to beat in all subsequent generations, forevermore.

*Every single life.*

## Worry?! Why?

Do you really think something could go "wrong"?
Are you not eternal? Have you forgotten how much
you're loved? Don't you see how far you've already
come? Could you possibly be in better hands?

Besides, your angels are so busssy right now . . .

# I know what to do!

I know what to do! Send me there!

Imagine me as a whirling ball of gold. Going in and out, to and fro. Healing, helping, soothing. Understanding, showing, mending. Bridging, rekindling, befriending.

Let me be your doctor. Let me be your lawyer. Let me be your ambassador. Your *Niña, Pinta,* and *Santa María.* Exploring, discovering, and lighting the way.

Because there's nowhere we can't go, there's no one we can't reach, and there's nothing we can't do.

*Hey, pretty cool to get those boats in there, huh? Huh? Huh?*

When you can't figure
out the hows, consider it a blessing, not a curse.
Because you cannot imagine how much freer it
makes you to simply dwell upon the end result,
without fear, without doubt, and without worry.
And really, that's what matters most.

You lucky salt.

Do you know why,
even here, way out in the Universe,
we love Fridays every bit as much as you?

Because on Fridays, all of the angels regroup and
share stories of the remarkable heroism, incredible
beauty, and heartfelt love witnessed all over your
astounding little planet.

*True, they do this every day, but on Fridays they
blast that "Let's get ready to rumble . . ." song for the
weekend. "Whoomp! There it is . . ."*

If I had seams, they'd burst.
Limits, they'd shatter. Doubts, they'd vanish.
Tears, conquered. Worries, shredded. Because I,
your faithful servant and doting guardian, who hears
your innermost thoughts, who walks in your shoes,
and who lingers in your breath, can hardly contain
the joy I feel over who you've become.

Of course, you have little idea of what
I'm talking about, but you will. And trust me,
you'll be overwhelmed, too.

Had to get that out, or I don't know what
else would have burst.

*Good thing I don't have stitches.*

It's not about what "they" do,
it's about what you do.

I'll deal with them.

*Trust me.*

Okay. Let's say you're walking

through the woods. All alone, miles from home, just minding your own business and lost in your own wondrous thoughts. Then suddenly, from absolutely nowhere, a huge grizzly bear literally "appears" on the path just a short distance in front of you, rears up on its hind legs, towering ten feet tall, waving both forepaws high in the air over its head, and roars. Immediately you see his large white teeth, his claws slicing the air, feel the heat from his breath in the cool morning air, and you feel your whole body spasm with fear as if you'd just been electrocuted. Nanoseconds seem like eternity. Your mind wants to shut down, but suddenly you regain control of the moment. Your adrenaline is pumping, your muscles are primed, and your heart is racing. Your instincts confirm what you feel in your heart: This "thing" is mad! It's scared! It wants to destroy you!

What do you do next?

*Freeze-frame.*

Okay. Now, let's say you're living your normal, everyday life. For the most part, you're a happy camper. Then suddenly, from absolutely nowhere, a huge bill appears. An important relationship stands on the brink of ruin. Your career of umpteen years is horribly threatened. Or you just plain can't seem to break through to "more." More of everything; abundance, health, or harmony. You're perplexed. You're angry. You're terrified. How? Why you? What gives? Your mind races. You want to put out the fires, throw a fit, wring a neck, and rail against an unfair world and the idiots who take you for granted. What do you do next?

*Freeze-frame.*

Do you see the similarities?

Do you see how engaging your "beasts," whether you fight or flee, only strengthens them and lures you deeper into their spell? That when facing a crisis or challenge, the thing to do is be still, go within, and turn your attention away from it? The exact opposite of what common sense would have you do.

Easy? No.

Lifesaving? Yes.

How? Practice.

# Speaking of bears . . .

You know how you're supposed to freeze if you startle one, or even drop into a fetal position? This makes you less threatening, and so the bear, after breathing down your neck and roaring like Tarzan, will leave you alone.

Well, what if, when you curl up, you remain terrified? (You will.) What if you doubt the effectiveness of your strategy? (You will.) What if you worry and wonder whether or not you're going to be the bear's next meal? (You will!)

Won't matter much, will it? Your actions will speak much louder than your fears, and the bear will quickly lose interest.

Do you see?

You needn't worry that you sometimes doubt, fear, or have limiting thoughts about living the life of your dreams, so long as you are also doing what you know to do.

Pretending is powerful. Very, very, very powerful. All reality is swayed, even manipulated, when you pretend.

So even if it feels silly (it might), even if you doubt its effectiveness (you might), even if you still worry about "bad" stuff (you will!), still, at least once a day, pretend that you're making progress, that you're provided for, and that all your dreams are coming true.

Bears and I have a lot in common. Easily fooled by those who pretend. Only instead of leaving you all alone, I'll commission the rest of the world to play along. It's the law.

For whatsoever you do
to further your dreams, I will do more.

# How can you know

that something hasn't worked out, unless you quit?

Ah-so,

The Universe

*It is working out, you are getting closer,
it is getting easier, and . . . you're looking absolutely
fantastic these days!*

# Welcome home, dear chap!

Welcome home! Yes, yes, I know all about it. That's right, wipe your feet at the door. Actually, there's a bath outside and you could use a good long soak. Don't worry. Take your time. This party never ends. Ah! Careful! You're dripping on this Note!

Oh, hi! Excuse me. Just welcoming back a fellow adventurer who, well, who had a nasty little spill in some Amazon quicksand. Help was on the way, but you should have seen him flail! Completely took him by surprise. And I do mean "took," which is quite all right. No coincidences, you know.

Hey, isn't taking the "quick" out of quicksand, or to paint a prettier picture, simply floating in a cool sun-drenched lagoon a lot like living the life of your dreams?!

The harder you physically work at it, the more you struggle to stay afloat, the quicker you sink. Takes some reverse logic to succeed. In moments of crisis—or bliss—instead of kicking and screaming and tossing out Hail Marys, remain calm and unflustered by appearances, stay focused upon what you want, and give unending thanks. Buoyancy, success, and the magic come automatically.

*Let me carry you higher. It's the only way to get there.*

# Do you want to know
what's really beautiful? Confidence.

Do you want to know what's really powerful?
Persistence.

Do you want to know what's really sexy?
(Please, I know about sexy.)
Not needing to be needed.

And if still "they" don't notice your good looks,
your strength, and your sashay . . .
could you feel more sorry for them?

*Who needs Botox?*

You aren't in time and space
to hit home runs. Couldn't even if you wanted to.
Can't be done. The logistics are impossible.
And besides, the pressure from trying would
overwhelm the hardiest of souls.

Home runs are what I do. You just pitch.

You want a new job, pitch it to me. You want
more friends, pitch it to me. You want to lose
weight, improve relationships, or strike it rich,
pitch it to me.

There's nothing you can throw that I can't hit
clear out of the park.

*Now, please, hand over the bat.*

# Okay, here's the skinny . . .

the answer to your question. The way, the light, the door. The most overlooked truth in reality. And the one that requires the most "uncommon sense" to fully grasp . . .

When it comes to effecting change (big or little, but especially big), manifesting the life of your dreams, or getting that perfect parking space, "thinking" is immeasurably more valuable when used to imagine what you want—the end result— than to figure out how you're going to get it.

*Which is why most people have to schlep through big parking lots.*

# A coincidence?

Do you think it's just a coincidence
that you look exactly as you do?

Do you think your height, the color of your eyes,
or the sound of your voice were accidents?

Do you think your insights into life, your gifts
of perception, or your sense of humor were the
result of random genetics?

No. You are exactly as you now are, with every
freckle, trait, and charm, because they all added
up to how you could make the biggest difference
with your life in time and space.

*And you're doing it.*

There's no one in your life
who hasn't always loved you.

They're all just learning how to show it.

Like you.

It's simply a matter of applying
what you have to what you face. That's all
that matters. Because by design, what you have
is always the greater.

Proudly yours,

The Universe

I've made up my mind
about your dream job.

Yep, it's all yours.
Once you make up your mind.

*Don't hate me.*

Material Abundance
is simply spirit, celebrating.

*By the way, it's also the inevitable consequence
of enlightenment.*

(in-ev-i-ta-ble: impossible to avoid or prevent)

# Fret not.

Time is on your side.

So are *all* the angels.

And "no" is never forever.

# Protocol Clarification

In the adventure of life there are no "Brownie
points" earned for suffering, sacrifice, or tears.
Nor for anguish, altruism, or selflessness.
In fact, you don't even get any for generosity,
gratitude, or compassion.

In time and space there are no
"Brownie points," period.

Might as well just do what makes you happy.

*Their cookies are a whole 'nother thing.*

## Adventurers Revelation

Here they are. The three pillars of reality. The only absolute Truths of Being. The bedrock of any awareness. The Holy Grail. They exist even without a belief in them and in spite of beliefs that contradict them.

First, there is only love.

Second, everything is of Me: one.

Third, thoughts become things.

Everything else, such as gravity, karma, relativity, and the countless others, are all subordinate and can be trumped, or even dispelled, by any one of these three Truths in the twinkling of an eye.

Can't imagine why I waited seven trillion years to share them. Maybe it was because it took seven trillion years before someone wondered. (You rock.)

Anyway, now you know. These are where I hide, like the wizard pulling levers behind the curtain in Oz. And now you know how utterly free, and powerful, and forever you will always be.

*Notice that only one contains a variable?*
*That's where you fit in.*

If at first you don't succeed,
it only means you're getting closer.

Avoid gray areas.

There, the illusion of safety is guarded by the lies of "maybe," "sometime," and "I don't know." There is a truth. There is a way. Life is absolute, and its principles exacting. If you put it out "there," it has to come back. Ask, and it must be revealed.

Think, speak, and move with your desires, and *nothing* will ever be the same.

# Long weekend?

Me, too. You know . . . war, chaos, and that new strain of bird flu. Guess I'm watching too much TV.

You probably won't believe this, but I'm as powerless as you when it comes to living other people's lives. A total zero. I don't even know what's going to happen tomorrow.

On the other hand, you are as powerful as I am when it comes to living your own. You decide what's meant to be. You can have anything you want. And everything is possible—flu or no flu, war or no war—shock and all.

Don't give away this power while waiting to see what happens to the rest of the world, when you can decide what will happen in yours.

The Universe

*See you in the news.*

# Heartbreak, disease,
### famine, and war casualties . . .

Can you imagine an angel who has only ever
known time and space from a distance, who
has spent the past few million years watching
humans live their passionate little lives—
helping them in and helping them out—
ever wanting to taste the bounty of creation
made flesh, herself?

Good. Now, can you imagine her insisting that her
life be perfect, squeaky-clean, without challenges,
without loss and the illusion of death? Or do you
see her being keen for the full-blown deal—
especially knowing that after each adventure she
would be together again with all the other angels,
in the palm of my hand?

Isn't it grand?

*Few choose to have their heart broken, to be infected with disease, afflicted by famine, or to die unexpectedly. And fewer still ever give these things any thought before experiencing them. But all have chosen and thought long and hard about the adventure of life. About being gripped by their passions and emotions so as to eventually learn of their divinity, to discover their power, and experience perfection. Unexpected "misfortunes" serve merely as bridges to such ends, like steps on a ladder, not leading to the end, but to new beginnings in a panorama of BEING too unbelievably expansive for human eyes to ever see.*

Hoping, wishing, and praying
shouldn't ever be confused with doing.

Know what I mean?

*As in, doing "all you can, with what you've got, from where you are."*

# A Paradoxical Perspective
## from your friend, the Universe

On earth it seems that most people fret, worry, and lose sleep over some of the silliest things they've done. But what's funny is that later on, from here, more often than not, it's the things they didn't do that haunt them.

*I'm not laughing, either.*

# You and I . . .

we're older than the sun, wiser than the moon, and deeper than the depths of space. We've always been together, we'll always be together, and until thy Kingdom comes and we are known as One, nothing will ever change this. Whatever you can imagine, I can make happen. Whatever you want, I already have. And for as long as you have thoughts to think, dreams to weave, and seeds to sow, NOTHING, for us, will be impossible.

What I'm trying to get at is, whatever you now want, I think we can handle it.

*Your dreams are what I've dreamed for you.*

Always, the best remedy
for dealing with a troubling past is
living in the present.

Hey! You're in time and space.
You're kind of like they are, so maybe you know what, I mean just exactly what, is going on with people these days?!

Maybe it has something to do with global warming, or could just be plain old plate tectonics messing with your "circuitry." I don't know, but more and more often I'm hearing claims of supernatural powers. I see folks dreaming like rock stars. And come prayer time, the "please may I"s and the "if it's okay with you"s are being replaced with *outrageously* high expectations. It's like they want it *all*!

Well, whatever it is, it's about *dang* time!

# Do you think

it would be as much fun if you could trade some of the happiest days of your life for not having to experience some of the saddest?

Do you think it would be as much fun if you could guarantee that some of your dreams would come true, by forgoing others?

How about if only your "good" thoughts became things . . . or would you still want it all?

Ha, I knew it! You take after me.

xxoo

There once was a time
in your very own history, long, long ago,
when the earth was a blooming paradise.
The diversity of life on the planet was as mind-
boggling as it was spectacular. Flowers sprang up
in the wild. Animals were loved as family members.
And complete strangers smiled and waved to one
another, as it was everyone's natural instinct to be
kind, to give, and to love.

Yep. Very, very little has changed since then.

See the good.

*Of course, back then they didn't have the
Discovery Channel, so few knew how
blessed they truly were.*

It's not the big dreams
I have trouble with, but the little ones.

Do us all a favor; think HUGE.

# Think of everything, all of it.

Every mountain before you, every pound you carry, every dollar you wish to manifest . . . as if it were made of pixie dust.

Suddenly—*dun, dun, dun, dunnnnnnn*— dominion over all things isn't so intimidating, huh?

*Like Beethoven?*
*You should hear his latest.*

In all my years as the Universe,
never once have I asked for anything in return
of anyone, anywhere, ever.

And I think that's a pretty good policy,
no matter who I am. Don't you?

Think less, feel more.

# What are you doing about it?

*Because it takes you doing what you can do, before I can do what I can do—you know, miracles and stuff.*

The trouble
with troublesome people is that they often have
much to teach to those they trouble.

Love 'em all.

If you have to ask for "signs,"
let this need of yours be a "sign" that you should
make haste very s-l-o-w-l-y.

# Report Card Day!
Here's your Report Card
from the "School of Life."

Compassionate—A+
(gives of self, even when no one's looking)

Intuitive—A+
(naturally gifted)

Ability to see from others' perspectives—A+
(practically goes out of body)

Spiritually alert—A+
(aura beginning to glow)

Resilient and adaptable to
unexpected change—A+
(like the Energizer Bunny)

Terminally optimistic—A+
(fast rebounder)

Exercises gratitude muscle—A+
(your cup to be refilled x 7)

Good-looking—A+
(a real hottie)

Patient and kind to self—hmmm, A
(could play a little more)

Visualizes every day . . .

Performs random "acts of faith" in line with
dreams . . .

You're amazing! Aced the very toughest courses in
time and space! Now, since the last two subjects are
the easiest, you get to grade yourself.

Okay, let's imagine

that the Universe is one big drive-thru McDonald's.
And let's say that one day, while tooling around,
you find yourself very, very hungry.

First, you drive up to the outdoor menu board,
decide what you want, and place your order.
The point? You HAVE to make a decision,
and place your order.

Second, you drive your car to window 1 and make
payment. The point? There's still stuff you must do,
even after placing your order.

Third, you drive to window 2 and receive your
"Happy Meal." The point? Your part is the easy
part, but you must keep on moving.

Point 4, you can always change your mind about what you ordered, and though it may be inconvenient, sometimes it's worth it.

Point 5, "Happy Meals" won't really make you happy. But neither will anything else you order, though the act, or journey, of willfully manifesting what you want totally rocks, and will eventually remind you of your divinity.

Point 6, when you get what you want, everyone wins.

Point 7, the Universe exists to serve you.

There are those
who absolutely think all the right thoughts.
Yet if they're not doing all they can, with what
they've got, from where they are, then you can just
guess what else they're probably thinking.

And those other thoughts are busy at work, too.

# Now be honest

and think of all your dreams that have already come true.

A lot, right? Tons.
Actually, you're a bit of a legend here already.

Now, do you remember how before all the big ones came true, when you were pushing, and reaching, and striving; hoping, wishing, and praying, you'd think to yourself, "Then I'll be freer. Then I'll be more confident. Then I'll know all things are possible! How happy I will be!"

Hey, what happened?

# It's working.

No, you probably can't see it yet, but I can. Wheels are now turning that have never turned before. Winds are now howling that have never howled before. And players from every walk of life are being drawn into place as if in some hypnotic dance. All because of you, your dreams, and your divinely stubborn persistence.

If I wasn't the Universe, I don't think I'd believe it.

*It's working.*

# I want you to think

of your life today, just as it is, just where you are.

Okay. Now I want you to think of the fabulous life of your dreams.

All right. Now, do you realize that getting from here to there is not something you can do without me?

I thought so. But then do you also realize that it's not something I can do without you?

Awesome, we're almost there! And do you further realize that the things I can do, you cannot? And that the things you can do, I cannot?

That's big.

*In your every pursuit after your every dream, I am there. I want for you what you want yourself. And always, I know the absolute fastest way to bring it about. But to use me, to engage the magic, you must first use yourself. Don't hesitate, be bold, have faith. Imagine, visualize, and commence living the life of your dreams today, to any degree that you can, and mountains will be the least that we'll move.*

NOTES FROM THE UNIVERSE

# Whoa . . .
did you mean for this to be happening? Did you
intend to change the course of history?

Do you fully comprehend the "ripple effect"?

Well, just so you know, these are the unavoidable
consequences of thoughtfulness, patience,
and unbridled kindness.

*I love it when you're wild and crazy.*

I didn't give you the power,
the glory, and the Kingdom so that you could just
"eke" by, be selfless, and make sacrifices. I didn't give
you dominion over all things so that just a few of
your dreams might come true.

I gave you these things so that you could have,
do, and be whatever you want.

*Comprende?*

## Alakazaam, alakazoo . . .

That should pretty much do it.

You're now wiser than you've ever been, younger than you'll ever be, and less likely to wish without taking action, pray without having faith, and hope without remembering the magic.

Ha! Who needs the lottery?!

Helps to know the Universe, huh?

*Now, please, remember your new skill sets.*

There's always been something
about you that gave me goose bumps and, finally,
I think I'm able to put a finger on it.

Without you, who else would the angels point to
when speaking of "our kind—only braver"?

You inspire us each and every day.

With deep pride,

The Universe

*No, I don't really have fingers.*

# Hup! Stop! Phew!

Glad I caught you early because today
is going to be "one of those days."

You know, the kind of day that will literally
unfold, moment by moment, phone call by
phone call, event after event, all based upon
the thoughts you choose to think, moment
by moment, phone call by phone call, event
after event, starting right now.

You are so powerful that the entire world
looks to you for direction. (Well, at least today,
because it is going to be one of those days.)

*Really, for you, today,
it's going to be like pulling rabbits from a hat.*

Don't all those goody-goodies
who tell you that life is "how you take it"
make you want to scream?!

Me, too, but let's have patience with them.

Life's not about how you take it, it's about the glory
of manipulating facts and crafting circumstances,
magnetizing players and forging alliances, leveraging
your wits and engaging the magic so that you can
have the sun, the moon, and the stars.

Full stop.

# Challenges and issues
## and problems.

Lions and tigers and bears. They're just me!
Showing up when you've somehow forgotten—
and need to be reminded of—how unbelievably
powerful you really are.

Because you will prevail.

Oh my!

*Of course, I could have just "drawn you pictures," sent
you to workshops, gotten you a tutor, but . . . oh, no. "I
want to be like the others. I want to make my own
reality. You said I could do it myself!"*

*Ahhhhh, to be the Universe.*

# The "word" of the week
## will be salamander.

Sa-la-man-der.

Hey, what's wrong with salamander?

Salamanders were one of my ways of becoming even "more" than who I was before there were any salamanders.

You know I could have picked armadillos, or tungsten, or pink, because I was less before each of them, too, but I picked salamanders. Maybe because as amphibians, they typically live in two worlds. Yeah, they live in two worlds: in water and on land.

Are you beginning to get my drift?

Do you see where I'm going with this one?

You're kind of like a salamander . . .
(no, not because you live on land)

Thanks for making me "more" in spirit and in flesh.

IOU Big.

Agh . . . ahem . . . excuse me,
but it's imperative that you read this one right away.
Lickity-split. Please . . . drop everything.

Have you ever thought to give thanks in advance
for not "losing" yourself when your ship comes in?
Seriously. For remaining grateful, considerate,
and inspired long after the floodgates open?
People often change, you know, once the magical
winds of fortune fill their sails. And sometimes,
it ain't pretty.

Well, not that anything is about to happen
(I never tell fortunes—prefer surprises), but let's
just say, hypothetically speaking, if incredible times
were just around the corner for you (or anyone
for that matter, I'm just using you as an example).

New friends. Bellyaching laughter. Skipping, dancing, and holding hands. A new fabulous home in the mountains (shhhhhh, this is just a "what-if," don't get carried away). I thought now might be a good time to tell you, how much I like you the way you are.

Close call.

*One can never be too careful when the magic is about to be unleashed—in general, you know. (So please, give thanks for not losing yourself in advance. There's not much time left!)*

# You know that feeling?

That sense of eagerness for the moment. Optimism for the future. And confidence that you are exactly "when" and where you should be. That feeling that makes dark days lighter and light days brighter. That precedes breakthroughs, conquests, and euphoria.

Yes, that feeling!

Well, it doesn't just come.

You have to give it to yourself.

Go on.

*If it helps, take it from me that you are exactly when and where you should be.*

# Okay, to clarify a bit:

You simply do not owe anyone, anything, ever.

Whoever they are, you are in their life because it served them. It made their life better. This is what they wanted. You are not in their life because they wanted to serve you. You can feel good about this. It's the ultimate compliment.

They are in your life because it served you. It made your life better. This is what you wanted. They were not initially, nor are they now primarily, in your life because you wanted to serve them. You can feel just as good about this. It makes the world go 'round. That's just the way it works.

And it's okay if and when your needs and theirs change. This also makes the world go 'round.

Hope that didn't hurt.

You're free.

*By the way, you've always made my life better.*

Oh . . . to see dreams abandoned
in the name of logic, for being unreasonable,
impractical, or pure fantasy, absolutely breaks
my heart.

But just as sad is seeing logic abandoned in the
name of dreams, with the sometimes overly
simplistic rationale that "anything is possible,"
"thoughts become things," "dreams come true."
Ugh.

Logic has its place. Not because it helps depict
the nature of reality (it doesn't), but because it can
help chart a course of least resistance through a
maze of sometimes hard-to-detect limiting beliefs,
thereby leading to an action plan, bolstering faith,
belief, and confidence, speeding up the whole
manifestation process.

For example, let's say you dream of crossing a
particular river that has a swift-moving current,
and in your mind you think it can be done in one
of two ways: you can either walk upon the water
(which you know is possible), or you can physically
train over a few months in order to swim it.

Now, how capable would you be of believing that you will ultimately achieve your dream (crossing the river) using either of the two ways? You'd be very capable. You'd believe, you'd immediately begin training, you'd find it easy to visualize yourself walking the shores on the other side, and it would be a done deal.

Okay, now how about if you were only allowed to walk upon the water (which is the predicament people create when they solely rely on the magic to carry them through life)? Would you believe in your dream of crossing the river? Would you be psyched? Or scared? Would you start moving toward your goal, or be paralyzed?

The funny thing is that in the first scenario, with your visualizing and believing (as evidenced by your preparations), "the Universe," depending upon your other beliefs, might intervene and whisk you across the river in ways you hadn't even known were possible, maybe even sending you a new best friend who could point out a nearby footbridge (I do that kind of thing, you know).

But for the poor chap who insists upon the magic carrying him across . . . Well, he's likely still sitting on the bank, chanting, and oommming, and visualizing. Burning incense, sporting henna tattoos, even telling passersby about the magic. But having a heck of a time truly believing that he can walk on water. The other funny thing is that having crossed the river via conventional methods, having mixed in a bit of logic with your approach, and having met with your inevitable success, now more than ever you understand that "anything is possible." That "thoughts become things." And that "dreams do come true." Far more so than the theoretical guru who still sits at the water's edge.

Sometimes it's spiritual to get logical. To do the obvious. To pound the pavement, knock on doors, spread the word. Besides, it sure beats just sitting around waiting to win the lottery. Expecting to meet your soul mate at the mall. Or planning to be discovered at Starbucks.

*If you're already walking on water, please just forward this Note to someone who's not.*

When all else seems to fail . . .
you can always help someone else, and succeed.

# You know, I think of myself

as pretty wonderful. So do many others. But I have to tell you that I still field a lot of complaints about the nature of reality. Can you believe it? I mean, life in time and space could not possibly be any easier, any fairer, or any more "bootylicious" than it is. But such is the lot of the Universe, and that's okay by me.

Chief among these complaints are from those who haven't yet won the lottery in spite of, they say, believing, visualizing, and acting as if. Here is what I tell them, and I share this with you because there are so many parallels, and perhaps one day—maybe, not necessarily, but maybe—some of this can be shared by you (when you start fielding these complaints yourself, of course).

Okay. I say to my people, "What you really want are bucks, dinars, or rupees, right? In a word, abundance, yes? Not to win the lottery." They say, "Yes, Universe." "And have I not often said, by way of many, many others, that you must do what you can do, all you can do, help yourself, if you want me to do what I can do, all I can do, to help you?

If you fish, go fishing. If you sell, go selling. If you teach, go teaching. Because such demonstrations show us (me and you) you're serious. They reflect a belief that you are not helpless, and they help you enjoy what you already have—taking your mind off of the lack. Right?"

"Yes, Universe."

"Now, if you want abundance, and you are as good-looking, and talented, and insightful, and resilient, and fearless, and powerful as you darn well know you are, yet all you're doing to experience it is buying lottery tickets, well . . . have I made my point?"

"No, Universe."

"If all you're doing is buying lottery tickets, then not only are you not doing all you can do, but this tells 'us' there are other issues going on as well that aren't being addressed. And hoping to dodge them by winning the lottery is just poor planning. Because when I finally do pick your numbers and abundance showers down upon you like there's no tomorrow and your every cup, bucket, and tub is overflowing with bullion, jewels, and Hummers . . . Very, very little will actually change in your life, and you'll discover that abundance was not really what you most wanted."

That's what I tell them.

Your Sugar-Buddy in Adventure,

The Universe

PS—"There are so many parallels."

(*bootylicious*: rap slang for "delicious," sort of)

So what if it takes a long time?
So what if it's already taken longer
then you thought?

So what if it will still take longer?

The day will nevertheless arrive, as it always does,
when all your prior efforts, determination, and
persistence will seem a paltry price indeed as
you are lifted irrevocably higher, as if by
chariots of fire.

I can hear the music now.

*I'm telling ya, I designed the system.*
*And by design, you have no idea, yet,*
*of the euphoric glory that draws ever near.*

What is it that
you'd really, really like to see happen in your life,
but have not visualized in a really, really long time?

Right!

Well, let's just say conditions are now favorable,
and it's time to rock-and-roll.

# Wherever you are drawn, go!

It's usually just me talking to you.

And the way you can be certain it's me
is that both your head and your heart will agree.

If it's not me, it's usually just laziness,
or pride, or fear.

"God," how I love you.

*By the way, there's no such thing as the devil—
and your heart has always known this.*

A word on miracles . . .
Don't let those that have not yet transpired,
blind you to those that have.

It really fouls things up.

*Besides, you're doing so well for yourself.*

Acts of kindness,
however small—a smile, a compliment,
a helping hand—plant seeds of hope, love,
and beauty in a spectacular garden you'll one day
call home.

*In the meantime, I'm enjoying the heck out of 'em.*

You might never guess it
but sometimes, even here, we get frustrated. The classic case happens at homecoming parties when we hear the guest of honor lament, "Gosh, but I had no idea! I never would have guessed! I didn't know I had such an affect on others! I didn't know I was so responsible for my thoughts, words, and deeds! I just didn't know . . ."

But it's even worse for them when we reply, "Yes, but you could have."

*Of course, we follow that up with something much lighter, like, "Hey, you look fab in wings!"*

# Let's get back to basics . . .

You live in a dreamworld where all things are possible. Your mere existence is the undeniable proof.

Hallelujah,

The Universe

Oh sure, you can knock
and it will be opened. Seek and it will be found.
Ask and it will be answered. But you could
also just say "thanks."

And believing, you'll see that that which
you stood in need of was there all along.

What a system, huh?
We call it built-in redundancy.

Would it make any difference
if you knew that we understand, deeply,
the battles you've waged? To know that we've
approved of the choices you've made? That you
have your own fan club here? That on the weekends
we watch movie clips of your life? That every single
morning we celebrate your birthday? That what
you've learned, you've taught us all?

Would it make any difference if you knew that
sometimes when no one's watching, we each,
in our own way, pretend to be you?

Well, whether or not it makes a difference,
you have.

Do you think if someone deeply believed that they and I were one—that I stirred in their heart, ran through their veins, and shone from their eyes—they'd wait for the part of me that existed "outside" of themselves to make their dreams come true?

Or would they seize each moment of every day, assured of their inevitable success?

Phew,

The Universe

*I work through you, not for you.*

It takes a BIG person
to accept full responsibility
for their own happiness.

It takes an even bigger person to accept full
responsibility for their own unhappiness.

But it takes a spiritual giant who, upon realizing
any degree of unhappiness, decides to be the change
they seek, in spite of having to endure the "same old,
same old" that may still linger on for a while.

Yeah.

Fee-Fi-Fo-Fum.

Throughout your entire life
you've moved mountains, averted disasters,
and orchestrated the most thrilling of comebacks,
clutches, and coincidences.

Hey, I should be asking you for help.

You know what's so strange
about walking that long, and oftentimes lonely,
road of life?

When you reach its end, you won't remember it
being either long, or lonely.

# Has it occurred to you

that just as much as you now want your dreams
to come true, once they have, you'll just as earnestly,
passionately, and "badly" want to do, be,
and have even more?

Of course it has.

So with this line of thinking, you also realize
that you will never, ever have all you want, right?
Oh, that's not so bad, it means as you constantly
achieve, so will you simultaneously invent new
dreams, just as you always have.

Brilliant.

So the trick, then, to being happy, is learning
to experience it even though you don't yet have
all you want, because you never will.

*Nail this, and you'll be set for eternity.*

# Wasn't it clever of me
to think you up? I mean, come on, wow!

Never has there walked the face of the earth someone who thinks with your degree of insight. Who loves with your degree of care. Or who feels with your degree of hope. And never has there been such a need for a soul with gifts like yours, because at this very moment there are people only you can reach, and differences only you can make.

*Yeah, I must have been having a really good day.*

# By the sacred powers

vested in me—by me—I've decided to share the Secret Plan behind Creation (the SPC, shhhh!) with the most able, competent, and noble adventurers ever to live. This way, there'll be no more waiting around by anyone expecting to be shown their purpose and mission.

Ready?

There is none.

How could there be, without limiting you?

Sorry. I can understand how that might tick some off. I mean, there's no one you're supposed to save. There's no hero or heroine destined to save you. And neither will the sky light up tomorrow with inscriptions as to what you should or shouldn't do.

That's the beauty of it. You decide these things, and you can choose whatever you like. But until you do, little else will happen, except that you may be buffeted about by the decisions of others.

*Choose your horse, stake your claim,*
*and move with it.*

## A Public Service Announcement
### from the Universe:

Be on guard against those who help others in the name of sacrifice, selflessness, or altruism, instead of in the name of joy. Because usually, they don't really help all that much.

*Sad is the life that gives without realizing how much, in turn, it receives.*

# You do know, of course,
#### why you're here—don't you?

Because you couldn't resist the challenge.

Nothing in all creation, not in any sphere of the Universe, compares to being born into time and space without any recollection of your past; having to find your own way when lost, your own courage when frightened, and the infinite powers at your disposal when challenged; left to the elements to rediscover your supremacy over them; driven by your passions so that you might rise above your humble, naked beginnings, and ultimately see through the illusions that had trapped you. To find yourself, once again, high upon the throne of thy Kingdom come, whence it all began.

*Either that, or you were dared.*

# Ever wonder

how some of those who achieve incredible success, amass fortunes, and enjoy sizzling relationships seem so unlikely? You know, they're not that smart, good-looking, or even creative.

It's because intelligence, looks, even creativity, come in a distant second place to believing. They achieved because they believed they would, and so the heavens and earth were moved.

*Whatever I've done for another, well . . .*
*just think of it as practice for what I can do for you.*

Enjoying short-term pleasures
at the expense of long-term dreams is just
about as foolish a strategy as pursuing long-term
dreams at the expense of short-term pleasures.

*Pursue both.*

# If you take care of the inches,
## I'll take care of the miles.

*You just have to go first.*

You've done better
than you know. You've helped more than you
realize. And you're closer than you think.

*Honestly, those poor Joneses.*

While it's often thought
that happiness may spring from having
some serious "bucks," it actually works best
the other way around.

Your celestial financial planner,

The Universe

*It's not a trick of brilliance, or charm. Not wit
or insight. Not health or prosperity or popularity
or depth. Happiness, alone, breeds happiness.
Just as it does all those other things.*

## As surely as mountains

are to be climbed and oceans sailed, your dreams are meant to come true. This is why you're here, to live the life of your dreams. Not to be tested, challenged, and tried, but to conquer, champion, and rule.

Keep going, forge ahead, press on, and the day must dawn when your thirsts shall be quenched, and you, exalted.

Don't ever settle for less, don't ever think it's too late, and never, ever, ever compromise a dream.

*If I didn't finally make that crystal clear, you'd throttle me once you got back.*

Don't doubt, hesitate, or waver.
There is no burden too great, no mountain
too large, and no goal too high, if you do
not doubt, hesitate, or waver, because the
only things that can derail a dream are
thoughts in contradiction.

No matter what happens
or doesn't happen. No matter where you go
or don't go. And no matter who you see or
don't see. Today, this week, this episode of
your life, will be looked back upon with the
deepest fondness because the time will come
when you will see its glorious perfection.

All right, the reservation's been made and a Beechcraft 400A private jet with experienced staff, advanced multimedia hookups for every passenger, and faux-leopard-skin sleeper recliners throughout, will be yours for any twenty-one days you choose. Just as soon as you arrange payment of US$368,750. In advance. Fuel, of course, will be extra.

Now, repeat after me:

"You have to be joking! Faux leopard skin is so 'early 2000.' What else do they have?"

Cool. Now stay with this perspective, because this kind of transaction takes place every single day for those who already have.

*And because perspectives summon circumstances that change fortunes.*

Can you imagine someone
waiting for a rosebud—yearning to smell its
heavenly fragrance and eager to see its impossible
beauty—yet becoming so focused and impatient
for its impending bloom that they become blind
to all the others that already have?

It happens.

Of course you can count on me,
but please, never forget, I'm counting on you.

## Here's a clue

on how to know when new experiences, like you've never experienced before, are about to transform your life, even when nothing seems to be happening.

For the first time ever, you start saying and doing things that you've never said or done before, even though nothing seems to be happening.

Especially the "doing" part.

# Do you know what
you've been doing your entire life?

No, besides getting better.

Nope, besides getting wiser.

Noooo, besides getting older.

My, you are talkative today.

You've been touching, teaching, and healing
friends and total strangers every step of the way.

Lay on thy hands!

The Universe

*And everywhere you went,
the flowers gently swayed.*

Problems only exist
when one looks to the physical world for solutions.

As if!

*As if you could change the story line of a movie by yanking on the silver screen.*

For those truly enlightened,
they have but to open their eyes upon making
a "wish" to see the entire Universe conspiring on
their behalf.

For those not so enlightened, it's the exact
same . . . except upon opening their eyes they
usually just see "stuff." And so they lose faith,
forget to give thanks, and are just too frightened to
"buy the shoes."

Pity.

# Go for it, not once,

but again and again and again. Whatever it takes. Because in the end, with arms held high in the winner's circle, beaming with joy, as light as a feather, crying your eyes out, you'll see how fantastically disproportionate the rewards are for the effort expended, the risks taken, and the price paid—no matter how many false starts you endured. And you'll be astounded at how quickly you made it, even though, when the going got tough and your spirits ebbed, you thought you'd never, ever, ever, "see the day."

*Oh "God," I'm so proud of you.*

All that you need,
to have all that you want, lies inside of you,
right now. Everything.

There are a million reasons
why any dream might be considered irrational,
unreasonable, and a silly waste of time.

On the other hand, I can think of one that blows
'em all out of the water . . .

We're in this together.

*There's no breath you take, or step you make,*
*that we don't share.*

If you only knew,
just how incredibly, wonderfully close you
already are to all that your heart desires . . .
you'd be even closer.

If that's possible.

What would you call a reality
that turned the page of every new day,
based entirely upon each individual's hopes
and fears, thoughts and feelings,
words and deeds?

How about "easy"?

You just never know
who in the crowd, standing beside you in line or
passing you in the street, might be raised in spirit,
or even lifted from despair, by the kindness in your
glance or the comfort of your smile.

But they may never forget.

*It takes so little.*

# There are some things

that are best forgotten. And when I remember
what a few of them are, I'll drop you a line.
But a couple of things worth remembering,
that are all too easily forgotten, are the times in your
life when you felt absolutely alone and uncertain.
Yet somehow, perhaps beyond perception,
there was a great *click*, after which, suddenly
a new friend appeared, an idea was imparted,
or a connection established, causing the tides
to turn and the floodgates to open.

And remembering this, should such "alone
and uncertain times" ever revisit you, however dark
they may seem, you'll at least be comforted by
recalling how transient they always are.

Pass it on,

The Universe

*Did you just hear something?*

## Would a "forever being"

ever worry about the future? Ever look back and wonder? Would a "forever being" ever have anything to fear?

Maybe. But only if they forgot they're forever.

When the hands of time are frozen and this world no longer exists, you'll just be getting started. This is preschool. Pre-pre-preschool. Let down your guard, go out on a limb, and take some more chances. Experiment, play, and stretch yourself. Honor your preferences, respect your wishes, and follow your heart. Practice, try, and try again.

Forget perfection, think adventure, and do all these things knowing that nothing can ever be taken away from a "forever being."

# Goodness, gracious,

what are people thinking about?! Dominion
over all things doesn't come with age, spirituality,
or even gratitude. In fact, it doesn't come at all.
You're born with it, and you now use it every
moment of every day, whenever you say,
"I will . . . I am . . . I have . . ."

And, for that matter, whenever you say,
"It's hard . . . I'm lost . . . I don't know . . ."

*Careful where you point that thing!*

You are exactly as you now are—
with your every mannerism, challenge, and trait;
skill, talent, and strength—because before this
life began, at the height of your glory, with full
awareness of your divinity, reach, and magnificence,
you knew best the choices that would maximize
this adventure. Bad hair and all.

Trust yourself. You chose superbly, and though
you may not see it yet, you've already mustered the
courage you had to muster, faced the fears you had
to face, braved the storms, fought the battles, and
exceeded every expectation you ever had for being
the kind of person you hoped you'd be.

Just tickles me pink,

The Universe

*I think I'm going to put you in charge of the planet.*

# Imagine taking a picture
with any old camera. You pretty much
just focus and click, right?

Now, does it matter how many friends are
seen in the viewfinder to find them all in the print?
Is it twice as hard to take a photo of two, or two
hundred, as it is of one? Does the camera work
harder to capture opulence instead of poverty?

Well, does it matter who takes the photo?
Whether they're spiritual or not? What kind of a
past they have? What their life lessons are?

Get the picture? I'm kind of like a camera.
I just copy what you focus on. And neither the
complexity of the subject nor the amount of
widgets it includes, nor where you've been in your
life heretofore, makes any difference.

Cheese,

The Universe

It's never too late.

There's no such thing
as too much gratitude. Because the more
of it you express, the more reasons
you'll be given to express it.

And as the "game" progresses,
you can rest assured that I will always "win."

Do you know why
butterflies flit? Fireflies light? Comets fall,
trees grow, cats purr, and tails wag?

Well, I have some hunches, and here's
my favorite: each is an aspect of the one who
perceives them, emissaries of self, disguised by the
elements, caught in an act of reflection, noticed in
just the right time and at just the right place, to
remind the dreamer, as if by metaphor, of their
own sublime miracle.

Kind of like you are, to me.

*Okay, so it's more than a hunch.*

To make hard tasks easy . . .
mountains molehills, and challenges simple,
you can opt for one of two paths. You can be still,
go within, wait for divine guidance, and expect
spontaneous enlightenment.

Or you can just roll up your sleeves and get busy
doing what you can, with what you've got,
from where you are.

May I suggest the latter? It's usually much faster.
And it makes you a bloomin' lightning rod for
divine guidance and spontaneous enlightenment.

*Sometimes the most spiritual thing you can do
is to get physical.*

Was just peering down through
your blue skies this morning. Unbelievable!
Do you see the same when you look up? Crystal
clear, azure, indigo, cobalt-kind-of-magical? There
really are no words for it. *Lovely* even pales. And to
think you get to live under it every single day of
your life, knowing that even with the cloudiest and
dreariest weather, just above the mist there exists
such iridescent splendor. As if to hint at what
forever might look like, to remind you of your
infinite reach, and to make clear life's perfection.
Because if such beauty can exist in the sky alone,
with only a palette of blue, imagine what else this
artist can do.

Sometimes, to be honest, it's all so beautiful
it makes my heart skip.

*Oh, dearie me, of course I have a heart!*
*And when it's not skipping or jumping for joy,*
*it's beating inside of yours.*

If, way down deep,
you can even slightly comprehend that time
is an illusion and that space is just a stage, then it
shouldn't take much of a leap to realize how
safe you are, how much magic there is, and,
most important, that there must exist a
superconsciousness with wishes and dreams
all its own . . . that include you.

*Let's get this party started.*

It doesn't get any more beautiful,
any more magical, any richer, or any easier
than things are right now.

Until, of course, you start expecting it to.

At which point,
I hope you have a really good broker.

*Expectation summons legions.*

## The Evolution of a Dream

Dream is implanted into brain.

Dreamer becomes thrilled.

Dreamer becomes terrified.

If no action is taken, terrifying thoughts
grow into flesh-eating monsters.
Dream is considered unrealistic.

If action is taken, terrifying thoughts are revealed
to be paper tigers. Confidence soars, miracles
unfold, and dreamer begins to saunter.

Either way, *nothing* remains the same.

*Act! The difference it will make in your life is
more than can be conprehended. But, of course,
this is also true of inaction.*

# The best shortcut

of all to the life of your dreams,
is knowing that you've already arrived.

Because you have.

Would there be any point
in giving you the gift of imagination, the freedom
to think as you choose, and dreams that set your
soul on fire if even a single one of them couldn't
come true?

I think not.

I love you too, too much.